To Gemma
+ Kelly

Hope this book blesses you
both on your journey
together

God Bless
Jennie x

Also by Jernine Russell

The NAKED Truth About Having A Baby

The NAKED Truth About Marriage

Jernine Russell

Published by

Dedication

There would be no book on marriage without my husband Marlon!

Thank you for being by my side for the past 19 years - 15, as my 'boyfriend' and four as my husband. Thank you for supporting me, encouraging me and for being my biggest cheerleader. When I feel like giving up, you are the reassuring voice reminding me to keep going, which was definitely needed during this journey.

I am so grateful to have found a love like ours; it is rare and special and makes my heart feel full.

You are the best teammate I could ever wish for and with you alongside me, I can win any game, race or overcome any hurdle.

You are my best friend, father of my children and king of our world. I love what we have built and continue to build together.

Let's continue to create memories together and leave a beautiful and powerful legacy of marriage for our children and grandchildren to come.

Appreciations

I am forever indebted to my family and friends who encourage, uplift and pray over me, and to God who has called me to and driven me to fulfil this purpose.

Let me first honour and acknowledge my Heavenly Father (who I fondly call Dad). Thank you for this assignment; it hasn't been easy or something I have received willingly (would I be me, if I didn't put up a little fight?). However, here I am, assignment completed. I am in awe of what you are doing in my life and how you are using this book to work, develop and strengthen not only my own marriage but also the marriages of many others. I believe that this book is the starting point for some restorative work and replenishment of relationships of those who are already married. May it also set a foundation and template for those preparing to get married, whilst giving food for thought for those who are separated or divorced.

So much thanks and gratitude for my remarkable husband Marlon. Marlon, I love you so much and am so blessed to be married to you. Thank you for choosing me and loving me. Thank you for our three wonderful children and for standing in agreement as we navigate the journey of parenthood. Let's continue to use our marriage to reassure others that marriage can work. Let's raise the standards of marriage and break negative cycles together.

I am so grateful for my children Reiley, Rae and Roman. You inspire me to be better, grow more, take risks, exceed limitations, love, laugh and live intentionally. You motivate me, improve me and challenge me in ways that are incomprehensible. You have taught me so much and I want to demonstrate that you can do *anything* you set your mind to.

Thank you to my parents Michael and Ana-Maria for your love and guidance. Thank you for the valuable lessons you have taught me. Mum, you are an exceptional woman who I am so proud of. You are courageous, strong, and an overcomer. Despite all the odds, you have provided a strong foundation for my siblings and I and we are eternally grateful. Dad, thanks for changing the narrative in my story and for working so hard to rebuild our relationship.

Thank you to my brother Bjorn and my sister Margaret; you are not just my siblings but also my friends. You enrich and enhance my life and make me feel that I can achieve anything!

Thank you to my grandmother Greta for your prayers and encouragement and for providing a true example of faith. In loving memory of my Grandad Leroy, thank you for loving Gran, making her laugh and demonstrating that marriage can work even when you're starting over in your 50s!

Thank you to my godmother Odette for being a consistent and unwavering support in my life.

Thank you to my friend Liselle for not only reading and providing constructive feedback for the book but for also being my right hand with all of the work for She Reigns over the past three years. You are the creative director, speaker, event co-ordinator… just to mention a few of your roles. Thank you for your brutal honesty and for pushing and pinching me to move beyond my comfort zone in all areas.

To Martin and Angie, thank you for our numerous conversations and prayers surrounding marriage.

Thank you Gran and Grandad, Auntie Patsy and Uncle Colin, Uncle Paul and Auntie Michelle, Vincia and Coldric, Jade and Jason, Val and Darren, Charmaine and Delwin, Crystal and Niyi and Sheliza and Leon for providing positive examples of marriage.

Thank you to Rhoda for your time and energy and encouragement, as well as your meticulous attention to detail to ensure the book was edited to perfection.

Thank you to Pastor Junior and Sister Sharlene - your prayers, guidance and wisdom are invaluable.

Pastor Mike Todd, Heather Lindsey, Myles Munroe, TD Jakes and Sarah Jakes - your sermons have inspired, challenged and 'grown' me in so many ways, that they have given me fuel to see this book through to fruition.

Foreword

I had no intention of writing this book but despite this, I felt compelled to, because of my belief in sharing our stories and personal experiences to benefit others. What I also have is a real desire to see marriage work.

I grew up in a single-parent household so never had a first-hand example of marriage. Though my parents were married they separated when I was two. Despite that, I always dreamed that they would get back together and we would live happily ever after (it never happened). However, not having a tangible example of the institution, as it is often called, gave me an unrealistic view of marriage. Despite that, even from an early age, I wanted to married, so much so that that when a boyfriend of mine told me that he never wanted to get married, I ended the relationship! For me a relationship had to have purpose, direction and a goal. Despite my early experience of my parents' marriage, I always believed that marriage can work.

There is nothing more that makes me happy than to see two people declare their undying love for one another. I'm known for watching wedding programmes and *Don't Tell The Bride*, *Say Yes to The Dress* and *Four Weddings* are a few of my favourites. Before getting married, my focus was on the dress and where I would have my wedding. It was only after getting married that I felt the urge to share some advice particularly about what a marriage is really about. From my experience, there is so much emphasis put on the wedding day and not enough thought, advice and support placed on what happens afterwards. What does it really take to preserve and sustain a stable and happy marriage?

Marriage is a covenant, an agreement between two people. There are declarations that couples make to one another during a ceremony. Do we ever refer back to these words again? Do we put as much time and effort into our marriage as we did in the early days of our relationship/courtship? Or even the energy and enthusiasm we did and had when planning the 'big' day? If we did this on a day-to-day basis, imagine how great marriage would be.

Like everything else in life, marriages have ups and downs and twists and turns. There are good times and sad times. When the sad times come, many couples often blame each other for the breakdown of the relationship. Very few take responsibility and accountability for what they bring to the relationship and what changes they can make or add to alter the dynamics of their relationship. What I hope to share with you in this book are some of my realities of what came after my big day. Let's explore The Naked Truth About Marriage.

The NAKED Truth About Marriage

The NAKED Truth About You

The NAKED Truth About Being Single

The NAKED Truth About Dating

The NAKED Truth About Living Together

The NAKED Truth About Finances

The NAKED Truth About Communication

The NAKED Truth About Arguments

The NAKED Truth About Trust

The NAKED Truth About Expectations

The NAKED Truth About Love

The NAKED Truth About Submission

The NAKED Truth About Growth and Change

The NAKED Truth About Sex and Intimacy

The NAKED Truth About In-Laws, Family and Friends

The NAKED Truth About Marriage According to Marlon Russell

The NAKED Truth About Marriage

The naked truth about marriage is that for it to work, for it to be a successful and happy one, a joint effort in hard work is essential.

My understanding of marriage is that it involves a great deal more than two people loving each other. My expectation of marriage was very much based on the fairy tales of hearsay, books, TV and films, especially as I didn't have an example from my parents. All this impacted on my ability to understand the realities of marriage. As a result, I was ill-prepared based on some quite unrealistic expectations. So, I now believe that if two people are coming together, they should be open and honest about what they want from marriage and what their expectations of the other person are. Think of it as a job with a job description. When you apply, you have to demonstrate how you meet the requirements of the role and responsibilities. When you get the job, there is an expectation that you fulfil those requirements and meet those responsibilities.

I believe marriage is similar and when you don't communicate what you need, want and expect, you run into difficulty or become frustrated. If you don't communicate that you need quality time every week, how can your spouse meet this expectation? The interesting and dynamic thing about marriage is that we are all different, so we have different desires. One of the best wedding presents my husband and I received was a book entitled *The Five Love Languages* written by Gary Chapman. It defines five ways that we express and experience love within a romantic relationship. The main message of the book is that if we don't understand our spouse's love language, we can be left with an unhappy partner which negatively impacts on the way they receive you or respond and interact with you. My husband Marlon and I were together for 15 years before getting married. We had experienced the usual ups and downs of any relationship, but reading this book was a complete 'game changer'! Once Marlon read the book and understood my love language, he began to communicate it, allowing me to feel loved and valued in a way I had never felt before. I too, was able to finally comprehend what he needed to feel secure and loved. I am not saying that we didn't feel loved by one another before. We had many happy years, but this book allowed me to truly understand him which in turn has allowed us to love each other more deeply.

The NAKED Truth About You

The naked truth about you is that you are a special and uniquely made individual.

You are shaped and formed by your upbringing, nurturing and life experiences. These all inform who you become and how you view the world impacting on how you interact with others in your relationships. The first relationship we have is with our parents. They demonstrate love and care (or sometimes the opposite) and we often mirror this. When you come together with someone, you bring to the table an enormous amount of experience and often, baggage. All the past hurt, pain, disappointment, joy, positive experiences and expectations are laid bare when you are in a relationship. My advice to you is therefore to spend time on you - get to know yourself, learn about what makes you happy, what makes you sad and know your strengths and weaknesses *before* you think of embarking on marriage. Learn to understand who you are and love who you are; if there are bits you don't like, work on them. Often if couples are getting married in a church, the church will offer pre-marital counselling which explores your relationship and its challenges and works to iron out any issues that may have arisen as a result. I strongly recommend this, whether that be individual counselling or couple's counselling; in fact, having both is ideal. This can open some necessary conversations and discussions and reveal anxieties or unresolved issues. Pre-marital counselling can also be a forum to discuss what your expectations from one another are after marriage. It is so important for you to share these with your partner, so they know the real you and how to love you.

Marriage is an amplifier so the issues that you had when you were single are often heightened during marriage. If you were insecure as a single person, marriage will not make your insecurities disappear but actually magnify them. If this is you, it is advisable to work on understanding and overcoming those insecurities. Perhaps read about trust or listen to a podcast exploring vulnerability. It may be that you need to have some talk therapy if there is an event that has been particularly hard to overcome such as a loss of someone close to you. Did you experience or witness domestic violence as a child or were you a victim of some form of abuse? Then you will need healing and some resolution or peace before you can share your life with someone else. If you are both broken, or have unresolved issues, please don't expect marriage to fix, complete or make you whole. The same can be said about your own unhappiness; many believe that marriage, or a husband/wife will magically make them happy. It will not – in fact, if you think about it, that is a lot of pressure to put on someone else. Your happiness is not your spouse's responsibility. It needs to come from within you and a significant other can only add to what is already there. Let's talk a little bit more about that life before marriage – the single life.

The NAKED Truth About Being Single

The naked truth about being single is that it is your opportunity to focus solely on yourself.

It is a season when you don't have to consider anyone else's needs but your own. It is a time for preparation, a developing ground. This time should be used to *become* someone and not *look* for someone. Singleness is a time for having fun, spending time with friends, learning a new skill, pursuing passions, studying and most importantly spending time with God. Use the time to sleep, travel, read, learn and spend time building and creating a strong foundation within yourself. It is good to go deep into you during this time. Explore your childhood. Are there unresolved issues? Did you experience any trauma? Look at your family background. What examples of marriage are in your family? Can you draw anything from these examples, good or bad? Think about what you would like in a marriage – what qualities would you like your potential spouse to have? What qualities do you have? What do you bring to the table?

What do you need to work on? What are your weaknesses – lack of patience, an inability to trust, feelings of rejection? If you discover things that need work, you should address them whilst single. The ultimate goal during this period of your life should be to work towards wholeness. There's an assumption that marriage is about finding your 'other half' or someone to 'complete you'. If that's what you are looking for, I'm afraid marriage will not give that. A relationship with God is your starting point to completing the work in you. Marriage is about two whole people coming together. Your spouse should add to you, complement you and bring another dimension to your already rich life.

Many who are single can find this chapter lonely, frustrating or can feel pressurised by family, friends or society to be in a relationship. I would ask though, would you rather be in a relationship where you are unhappy, stifled or abused, just to say you're in one? Marriage is not about rushing or settling for something just so that you can say you are married. I think it is for this reason that there are many separated or divorced people who, in the lead up to the wedding, knew that they were not doing the right thing; they probably knew the person wasn't right for them or that they were not ready. They were probably driven by the *need* to be married rather by being ready to do so. So, it is important to use the time when you are single as preparation to gain wisdom and understanding of yourself and the kind of person that would complement you.

The NAKED Truth About Dating

The naked truth about dating is that this is the getting to know you stage where you learn if you are compatible and whether there's a 'connection'.

This is the wining and dining stage, or what is usually referred to as the 'honeymoon' stage when everyone is wearing their airs and graces and are on their best behaviour. Everyone pulls out all the stops to impress and win over the person that they are dating. However, this is the perfect opportunity to carry out all your research about whether you can build a life with this person. I also say that during this time, whatever you do should be sustainable throughout the relationship and the subsequent marriage.

There are many people who believe that this is the hardest part whilst others find it the most enjoyable. I loved this part, from the feeling of butterflies in your stomach to choosing the 'date outfit'. Date night, where we might book a nice restaurant and dress up, is still a regular feature in our marriage even after 19 years. Many people stop doing these really important things. Why is it important? Well, because it is about taking the time and effort to plan and prioritise your spouse, focusing on them and giving them your undivided attention. It is even more important if you have children. Those who don't take time to 'date' whilst they are raising children often grow apart because they simply don't spend time with each other and then find that they no longer have much in common.

Dating is quality time spent conversing, laughing, enjoying each other's company and pursuing mutual interests. It is a time to put aside the monotonous day-to-day conversations about bills, children, what's for dinner and who didn't do the dishes. You can go out or stay in. It can cost hundreds of pounds or nothing at all. A walk together or a picnic in a park cost next to nothing. All that's needed is your imagination.

You have to date your spouse in marriage with the same effort and enthusiasm that you did when you were trying to 'woo' them. How else can you keep them if you stop doing what you did to get them? Keep them encouraged, energised and interested. Think of it like watering a plant. A plant only thrives when watered. In the same way, a marriage will only grow if watered with an investment of time, money and effort. What does this look like? Calling your partner throughout your day just because, sending a text message to say, 'I love you', bringing home a bunch of flowers for no reason, a foot rub or making dinner. These are just a few of the many and simple things that keep a relationship energised.

The NAKED Truth About Living Together

The naked truth about living together is that it is something that requires patience, communication and a lot of adjustment.

Living together involves sharing your personal and intimate space with someone else and it is important that you not only learn but also understand how to do this. We know how difficult it can be to share space with your parents or family, let alone your partner. It can push your tolerance to another level as it is about trying to align with someone who may not share your beliefs or habits when it comes to washing the dishes, making the bed or the position of the toilet seat!

Living together is transitional and as such requires change, adapting, communication and compromise. It is where you can agree on the practicalities and logistics within the household such as which side of the bed belongs to whom, how to share the space in the wardrobe, cleaning and who puts the bins out. From my experience, it is good to discuss what the traditions and patterns were in your respective households growing up so that you can talk about and ultimately decide how to do things in your household. This is important because your upbringing and expectations in this area may be so different and even conflicting, so if not put on the table, they can potentially cause issues later on in married life.

The division of labour and sharing of responsibilities are probably the most important areas to address practically. Who will pay the mortgage or rent – will it be shared or is the expectation that the husband is responsible? How will you divide the other bills? Who will do the food shopping – will this be done together, or do you take it in turns? Marlon and I share the cooking and cleaning in our household and we each cook on alternate evenings. I wash the clothes and primarily do the food shopping (when he comes with me, the food bill increases by at least £20 with all the 'extras' that he buys)! He puts the bins out and mows the lawn. We also take turns to wash the dishes, although this was the bane of the majority of our arguments in the early days of living together. We had many discussions and disagreements about this. Eventually, we agreed that whoever cooked should not have to wash up and this is something we have maintained up to now.

Just figure out what works best for your household. You also have to be willing to check in with one another to see what is working or not. Be open to compromise so that your household can function effectively.

The NAKED Truth About Finances

The naked truth about finances is that it is one of the major causes of marriages breaking down.

Our relationship with money is shaped by our parents or those who raised us – even if they didn't actually teach us anything, that also shapes our view on money. The financial habits or patterns we develop stem from this and have an impact on how we view and tackle finances within our marriages.

One fundamental and key step is to establish whether or not finances will be joint. Should you have a joint account to pay for household outgoings? I have known couples who don't combine their finances and still believe that what's theirs is theirs. In my opinion, this is a very rigid and selfish way to approach finances in marriage. When two people come together it means joining everything, including finances. The way in which this is done is of course personal, but there must be some unity.

Money and how it is handled is a shared responsibility where people should be honest and transparent with one another. So for example, if one has debt prior to the marriage, this should be discussed, and a plan made to pay it. When there is dishonesty and secrets in finances, problems are sure to arise. If you cannot be open about such matters, how can you expect there to be trust and intimacy in other areas of your marriage? Work out an approach to joint finances and stick to it.

One of the other difficulties in this area is in making financial decisions. These decisions should always be discussed and made together. If making an investment, both parties should be in agreement; the same goes if taking out a loan or in relation to anything else that may have a significant impact – positive *or* negative – on your finances.

Although my parents separated when I was very young, one of the things they both told me was that they shared everything. If my dad had £10, £5 was for my mum and £5 was his. 'One hand can't clap' is a saying my mum still tells me today, meaning that two people have to work together. Working together also means that the financial burden is shared.

The NAKED Truth About Communication

The naked truth about communication is that it is crucial if a relationship is going to work.

Communication, by definition, is the 'imparting or exchanging of information by speaking or writing to express your ideas, thoughts or feelings to someone else'.[1] In a marriage, the ability to communicate with your spouse is essential. Many challenges and problems in marriage arise as a result of either difficulties in communicating or just a lack of communication.

When you think of a young child who has yet to learn to speak, there are often tears and tantrums primarily because they cannot express their needs and desires. This too can feature in marriage. If one spouse can't express their feelings, they too become frustrated. If one can communicate but not in a way that the other can comprehend, that can lead to conflict. Another cause is perhaps when one can communicate but the other doesn't listen or allow a space for them to do so. Listening is crucial to communication.

There is the saying (and title of a book), 'Men are from Mars and women are from Venus,' that I came to understand when thinking about the ways in which men and women communicate. I had always considered myself to be a good communicator whilst Marlon, on the other hand, was someone who internalised his feelings. When I shared my feelings with him, his response was to put up a wall. He would either continue watching TV and ignore me, or even walk away, leaving me feeling angry and frustrated. What then happened over the years was that I stopped telling him how I felt, keeping it in until I exploded – the way a fizzy drink does after the bottle has been shaken. Then I would tell him about something that had upset me months before, which he most probably didn't remember. When he didn't respond, I'd phone my friend and vent instead of addressing things with him. I spent years holding in things just to avoid those awkward conversations where he didn't want to hear me; I'd then have a complete emotional meltdown because he didn't (another thing he found difficult to deal with). The turning point came when I started counselling. After a few months, I felt like I was in heaven, having someone to open up to and who would listen. Counselling identified an issue that I had when it came to expressing myself in situations that I sensed could be confrontational. I had to learn not to worry about what the other person may think or feel, but to express my feelings regardless. I took this approach with Marlon and when he did or said something that offended or upset me, I told him and explained how and why it made me feel that way (you have to use wisdom and not 'nit-pick' everything little thing your spouse says or does though). This did wonders for our relationship. I also chose the moments when I raised any issues so that for example, we weren't having a sensitive discussion when he or I was doing something else.

One piece of advice an uncle gave was, 'Don't go to bed angry with one another'. This brings to mind the scripture, *In your anger do not sin: Do not let the sun go down while you are still angry* – Ephesians 4:26. [2] To be honest, this can be challenging for me as I am stubborn (as is he!); despite this, I have stuck to this principle and will apologise or resolve things even when I have not felt at fault. The lesson for me is that marriage doesn't keep scores; it is not you versus your spouse. You are on the same team, so you have to score in the same goal, which means it doesn't matter who's right or wrong. It is all about whether you maintain harmony in and respect for the team.

The NAKED Truth About Arguments

*The naked truth about arguments is that **all** relationships and marriages have them. They can actually be the catalyst for change.*

In any healthy relationship, there are bound to be arguments; by definition, 'an argument is an exchange of diverging or opposing views and is typically a heated or angry one'.[3] I remember in the early years of my relationship with Marlon, we would argue over silly things, usually domestic stuff. We wouldn't speak for days or weeks on end, never discussing what the root or real issue was. One of the difficulties was that no one wanted to back down or apologise. There were occasions where he would walk out of the house during an argument and I would get so upset and try to stop him from leaving, infuriating him more. One day, I asked him why he did that and he said he just needed to calm down and have space to think before he came back to the matter. I told him that his walking away felt personal, like he was walking away from me and not coming back.

I grew to understand that when he knew he was getting to his boiling point, he needed his space and his walking away was not leaving because he always came back.

Arguing can be healthy if you actually discuss what needs to be discussed and come to an understanding or resolution. Internalising things leads to outbursts like I used to have. Nevertheless, different people handle things differently when they are upset or annoyed; Marlon goes into his 'cave' where he becomes quiet and withdrawn, whereas my approach is 'let's discuss and get to the root of this problem.' My way may be informed by the nature of my work where I talk to people every day and encourage them to talk about their feelings. So it is easy for me to apply this to other situations. I also have experience of counselling and have seen the benefits of open communication and listening. However, we have had to accept and appreciate our different styles of communication.

The thing with arguments is that at some point, someone has to acknowledge their wrong or misstep, usually with an apology, before both parties can move forward. My marriage has shown me that sometimes you need to say sorry, even if you don't think you were wrong or at fault, in order to bring peace back into the home. Marlon is brilliant at creating a diversion when an argument is on the horizon; he tickles me or licks my face and I collapse in fits of laughter; there is no way I can stay mad after that!

When arguments are not resolved, problems will continuously arise within the marriage; the issue will no doubt rear its head again. Seeking counsel from a mediator or relationship counsellor can be beneficial if it is impossible to fix things between yourselves. It can help your spouse to feel heard as well as explore both sides of the argument in detail. The independent help can give a new perspective that can lead down the road to resolution.

Ultimately, marriage is about winning together, not against each other. You are a team fighting together against a situation.

Don't default to getting one over the other during arguments or difficulties – that's not for marriage. Join forces and fight as one against what threatens your marriage.

The NAKED Truth About Trust

The naked truth about trust is that it is like a piece of paper - once you screw it up, it is never the same.

Trust is something that is built over time. It is earned through different experiences and situations during a relationship. Trust is an attribute that is necessary in marriage. If absent, the cracks will soon appear. Trust is 'the belief that someone will not harm you, or that something or someone is safe and reliable'.* Our ability to trust is learnt at a young age and is developed through our experiences. If the significant figures in your life broke your trust, it can make you less willing to do so with someone new.

If you enter marriage without trust in your spouse, being married will not magically create it. Instead, accusations and insecurity will thrive. Imagine how frustrating it would be to be constantly questioned about your whereabouts or movements. Similarly, no one wants to be repeatedly accused of imagined misdemeanours. Trust means being vulnerable and this can be extremely difficult if you have been hurt before. On the other hand, it is really hard for someone else to have to pay for your previous hurts. If an ex-partner betrayed your trust, it does not mean that your new love will do the same and to accept this means opening oneself up and allowing someone in.

I recall that in the early days of our relationship, I always kept my guard up and my husband later said that he found me really cold. This was a shock for me as I always had and still do describe myself as being warm and open. When what he'd said sunk in, I realised that my previous hurt was preventing me from letting him in. From that day I decided to work on letting my guard down so he could see the real me and not be scared of being hurt or let down. I truly trusted him; it was a gamble that I can happily say paid off.

The NAKED Truth About Expectations

The naked truth about expectations is that when they are not met, we are left feeling disappointed.

I think it is crucial to discuss your expectations for marriage *before* getting married so that your future spouse knows what is expected of them; likewise, you also get to know what is expected of you. Expectations have to be laid bare and worked through with compromise from both sides to make them realistic before *and* after the wedding! The expectations we have on the role of the husband and wife are probably top of the list.

Our expectations on roles will be based on our experiences and influenced by examples of our parents and other relatives, as well as peers. For example, your father may have been the breadwinner in your family so your expectation might be that this would be the same for your husband. Or you may have grown up seeing your mother do all the cooking and never seen your father in the kitchen, so you may have an expectation that your wife should be the one to prepare all the meals. Each marriage brings together two different people with different expectations and only the both of you can work out what works best for your household in order for it to run smoothly.

Marriages usually break down when our expectations are continually not being met. Feelings of unhappiness or resentment can build up as a result. All is fuelled by a lack of communication – about the expectations in the first place and the feelings that arise when they are not met. It is a vicious cycle that if not broken leads to the end of harmony, respect and commitment to making a marriage work.

My initial expectations of marriage were unrealistic as I had no real life basis from which to inform them. I could only formulate them based on what I saw from the periphery of other people's unions and fictional portrayals in TV and film. Then, I didn't communicate my expectations prior to getting married probably because we had been together for a very long time before we got married. However, this did not and should not make a difference – marriage is a separate entity from living together. It is important to talk about your *actual* expectations and your understanding of what marriage means. Then, talk about different circumstances and how you handle them may differ within marriage. Think about children, problems with infertility or surprise pregnancies, redundancy or promotions, illness and even death. All these new scenarios, challenges and changes can put a strain on or change the perspective of the marriage and thus, expectations need to be revisited, reviewed and adjusted throughout your marriage.

The NAKED Truth About Love

The naked truth about love is that love is a verb, an action, a doing word; it is something that is demonstrated, not just spoken.

Love is defined as 'an intense feeling of deep affection, or, a great interest and pleasure in something'.* Based on this definition, I am of the view that love is not fixed in the way in which it is experienced. It is a unique and special feeling that individuals embrace and express in a variety of ways. The way in which you love, feel love and give love is based on your own experience of receiving love.

So it makes sense that our childhood has a great impact on our understanding of love. Whether the way in which love was given and received was negative or positive, it goes on to impact the love we demonstrate to others. When love during our childhood is not given freely or is lacking, this can have devastating effects. When the love received during childhood is positive and rich, this is more likely to lead to fulfilling relationships where love is given and accepted freely.

Freud, a psychologist well known for his psychodynamic theory, explored the relationship between mother and son and father and daughter. He suggested that a young boy's love for or the relationship with his mother impacts on how he goes on to love as a man. Equally, a girl's first love is her father, and this relationship impacts and sets a precedent for how she loves or the way she expects love from a man. There are many other theories which oppose this of course, but it makes sense that an absence of these parental figures will impact on subsequent romantic relationships.

Looking back, I can identify some difficulties that arose from the estranged relationship I had with my own father in my formative years. Fortunately, my early experience of love didn't significantly affect my ability to love Marlon.

What I like most about love is someone being able to love the unlovable parts of you, and you theirs... you know, the annoying traits and weaknesses. For me, because I have felt and received God's love I have learned to love freely without restriction.

Love requires taking risks, being vulnerable, trust, honesty and so much more. Even if your experiences of love have not been positive, you are still worthy of giving and receiving it. When you have been hurt, you have to be careful that you do not accept love from the wrong people or push love away from the right ones.

The love you have for yourself determines how you allow others to treat and love you. So, this is the basis and foundation you need to build from. Often, whether we are aware of it or not, it is when we don't love ourselves that we welcome the most destructive and damaging people and relationships in our lives. Love for self ultimately is the most important to create before you can share it with another.

The NAKED Truth About Submission

The naked truth about submission is that 'man is the head and woman is the neck'. The head cannot move without the neck.

The Cambridge dictionary defines submission as 'the act of giving something for a decision to be made by others'. Submission within marriage is described as when a wife willingly and voluntarily chooses to submit herself under her husband's leadership and authority. I believe that we are often misled about the meaning of submission. Submission is usually viewed negatively and can be deemed sexist. However, submission requires trust as well as good leadership. If a man does not know what he is doing, or where he is going, how can he expect someone else to follow his lead? Submission requires you to relinquish control *but* relies on the two people within the marriage communicating to ensure that the direction they are heading in is where both want to go. *Sub* – means under, and *-mission* means an important assignment given to a person; therefore, a woman is part of the man's mission. Whoever you marry, you are connected to in order to fulfil God's purpose or mission. If you marry the wrong person, this can take you off the course to your own purpose. It is important to get to know someone and find out what his or her purpose and mission is to see if it is aligned with yours. God works all things for his good, but it is also up to you to recognise what is good for you.

Submission is an area that I have always struggled with. I am not sure if it is because I was raised by a fiercely independent woman who was raising me single-handedly; she had to take on all types of tasks and roles: decorating, fixing the car, cooking, cleaning, disciplining us and working numerous jobs to pay the bills and keep a roof over our heads. With no male figure in our home, I never saw my mum submit to anyone. She made the decisions and she had the vision and foresight for our family, so this is what I learned to do. The other reason that I think I struggled with submitting to my husband was because initially, I found it hard to trust him. This was not because I felt he was going to be unfaithful but I could not be sure that he would have my back and not let me down. I had never had such an experience from a man. With time, the trust grew, as through different situations he proved to me that I could rely on him. My relationship with God has had a significant impact on how I see submission as part of my marriage too. The more that I have grown to love and submit to God, the more he has taught me and demonstrated his love for me. In turn, I have learnt about reliability, trustworthiness and dependability. This has encouraged and allowed me to do the same in my marriage.

Here is something else to consider. Marriage described in the Bible mirrors the relationship and love between Christ and the church. When a husband submits to the Lord, he sets an example and the wife can confidently submit to him. As she leans on her husband and trusts him, so does her husband lean on God. The world's view of marriage and submission is contrary to the biblical view. You need to determine which view you are going to use to set the precedent in your marriage.

Prior to getting married, I did not understand the true meaning of submission. Since I got married, as my relationship with God deepened, it enabled my relationship with my husband to grow and so submission to him became easier. At the same time, becoming husband and wife led me to a closer relationship with God which in turn has benefited my marriage in many areas including that of submission.

The NAKED Truth About Growth And Change

The naked truth about growth and change within marriage is that it is inevitable; it is healthy so embrace it.

If you or your spouse do not change during your marriage, then something's wrong. You hear people say things like 'I don't love him anymore because he's changed,' or 'We are having issues in our marriage because she's not the person I married.' Change and growth are key in life – nothing and no one remains the same. As you grow older and have new and different experiences, these shape and mould you, so you must change. What is sometimes difficult is if one person in the marriage is evolving while the other remains stagnant. It can become frustrating if you are the one changing or moving forward and the other person is not; however it is important to understand that you *cannot* change anyone else, nor do people change at the same pace. You only have power and control over making changes to you. At the same time, it is important to complement each other's growth, meaning you support and embrace each other's evolution, especially if this change brings the other joy.

If you are married to someone that you want to change, you may be fighting a losing battle. You can talk, encourage, guide, motivate and support, but you can only change yourself. Your change may *inspire* them to change but you cannot *make* them change. All you can do is 'be the change, you want to see'.

Marlon and I have been together since our early twenties. I am definitely not the same person I was when we met. My foundation is the same, but I have grown through my experiences of studying, working and becoming a mother. The biggest transformation has come through my deepening relationship with God. I have experienced failures, losses and hurts which have shaped who I am today but that relationship has remained a constant source of inspiration and strength. One of my favourite sayings is 'I strive to be better than I was yesterday.' I am proud of the person I am and continue to become. Recently, I completed training to become a counsellor; it was the first time I had studied in years and since the birth of my youngest child. It took me out of the house, but Marlon was so supportive and was in fact inspired to study again too. During the process and throughout our relationship, we have shared new knowledge with each other, and not only have we shared but we have also applied what we have learnt to our own relationship. I previously mentioned the book *The Five Love Languages*. In actual fact, we both read it, and used it to shape the way we show our love for each other. It made us more intentional with our marriage.

With this experience, I would encourage you to welcome change and growth within your marriage for the long-term benefit for your relationship. Your spouse should 'water' your growth just as you should water theirs.

The NAKED Truth About Sex and Intimacy

The naked truth about sex and intimacy is that though separate entities they are inter-related.

Sex is defined as a 'physical activity in which two people become one and participate in to arouse or attempt to arouse each other sexually'.[4] Sex between two people who are not married can be exciting and enjoyable; however there is something special about sex, making love to someone that you love, trust, are committed to and understand. Within marriage, sex does not have to be a competition or performance. It becomes a selfless act whereby your spouse wants to make the experience about you, pleasuring you and attending to your needs and desires. In a marriage you can learn to understand and explore each other's bodies through body language and foreplay. Some people are put off marriage because they will have to spend the rest of their life having sex with the same person. What they may not realise is that the beauty of sex within a marriage is that there are layers and dimensions of the relationship that allow for exploration, variation and experimentation. It can be the most amazing, pleasurable and meaningful thing because you are exploring in trust and security. My experience is that as my connection with my husband has become deeper our sexual relationship has also intensified.

Just like everything else in marriage, I think it is important to communicate with your spouse about your expectations about sex. What is your 'normal'? Is it sex every day or is twice a week enough? What do you like and what's a turn off? Though sex is not the most important aspect in a marriage, it is a vital component and if it is missing, then this can cause significant issues.

Intimacy is defined as 'mental, emotional or physical closeness – knowing someone deeply and feeling known in all your being'. Intimacy is built up over time and requires patience and effort. It involves being open and talking through your thoughts and emotions, being vulnerable and showing someone else how you feel. You can have intimate relationships with your friends too.

There are *five levels of emotional intimacy ranging from level 1 which is about safe communication, like the general chit chat you have with a stranger in the supermarket, to level 5*5 where needs, emotions and desires are fully expressed. Intimacy is an area of contention for many marriages. It requires that you truly know someone and if you don't, there is a limit to how close you can get. I have heard people say you should marry your best friend and I understand this implicitly when it comes to intimacy. Your best friend is someone you know fully and with whom you can be truly yourself. They know you better than anyone else and you can share the fears, triumphs and deepest secrets that you wouldn't with anyone else. With this person, there is a level of vulnerability that no one else knows or sees. There is no pretence. They know your weaknesses and flaws and despite all that, they still love you. This is not something to be taken lightly and is something that's rare.

I've often heard men say that they have less sex in marriage than when they were single or dating. This may be due to the absence of intimacy within the marriage. In order to sustain a healthy and loving marriage, sex requires intimacy, which in turn, requires communication, patience and understanding. There may be times when one spouse doesn't feel like they want sex, but this should not lead to a feeling of rejection. With intimacy, it is still possible to have pleasure in the absence of sex. It does take work to develop and maintain a level of intimacy though. Couples who work long hours, focus all their attention on raising their families and stop spending time together lose that portal for intimacy; conversing, laughing, holding hands, giving massages, talking about desires and dreams, can all keep that connection when sex is less frequent than you would like. The importance of intimacy is seen when because it is lacking in a marriage, one or both seek that in someone outside of the marriage. For this reason, it is important to keep that portal open through spontaneity, excitement and nurturing that connection with your spouse throughout a marriage. Always aim to give your spouse the attention they require and deserve.

There is something to be learnt from the Bible on this subject too. It speaks about not having sex before marriage and I believe that is because God really wants us to spend time to grow intimacy – learning and getting to know your future spouse and yourself on a mental and emotional level before becoming physically intimate. There is therefore some truth to the concept that 'good sex starts in the mind!'

The NAKED Truth About In-Laws, Family and Friends

The naked truth about in-laws, family and friends is that they are not in your marriage.

Your marriage is sacred and should only involve you, your spouse and God. No one else belongs *in* it. You wouldn't want your spouse bringing another woman into your marriage and this applies to his mother too! Your spouse should remain first, ahead of anyone else. This is one of the expectations that we all have but do not necessarily abide by. Ephesians 5:31 says, *For this cause shall a man leave his father and mother, and shall be joined unto his wife, and they two shall be one flesh.*[6] A husband and wife become *one*. This means no one else, not even a mother or father, is a part of the union.

I think it is important to have an in-depth discussion about this before marriage with both your spouse and family. When married, it is also important to be mindful of who you confide in about your marriage as by doing so

63

you are bringing the other party into it. You have to remember that your relatives may be biased if you disclose an argument you've had with your spouse. Likewise, intimate conversations about the marriage is a recipe for disaster if it is with someone of the opposite sex. I am not opposed to having a supportive and loving network of family and friends, but this requires boundaries. Marlon and I have incredible support from others that brings encouragement and a great deal of love, not just for us but also for our children. They provide wisdom and can offer (and note, *offer*) advice about matters but it is for us to decide how we apply this advice. There is an important balance to be struck and boundaries to set.

Don't allow others to disrespect, put down or belittle your spouse in front of you. Defend them and let others know that they can't engage in that type of behaviour. Friends are a great source of laughter and fun but there's a line to be drawn when it comes to the interplay with your marriage. Both parties need to remember and remind friends that they're no longer single, and access is somewhat restricted. Those restrictions are to be defined and agreed with your spouse. If you do discuss matters or issues of your marriage with others, ensure you are seeking advice from a reliable source; that is usually someone who is also married. Your single friend may be a great friend, but that does not mean they are the best person to seek advice from about marriage. Use wisdom and good judgement.

The NAKED Truth About Marriage According to Marlon Russell

I never had the romantic vision that marriage conjures up for many. Never had the need or want to walk down the aisle. Never pictured me in a sea of confetti, holding hands, entering the archetypical white Rolls Royce with the 'Just Married' sign on the back. However, three kids down the line, a growing spirituality and the overwhelming want to make my 'girlfriend' (which was beginning to sound ridiculous!) happy and legitimate changed all that.

The funny thing is, I believe that marriage has had a more profound effect on me than on Jernine. See, even though my expectations of marriage were not exactly low, I did feel that as we had children together, lived together, had mortgages (not together!), then nothing was really going to change. On the other hand, she had all these pre-conceived notions that had been born from those schoolgirl chats in the playground. So, without a doubt, the expectations were all hers; for me, I expected it would all be business as usual!

Things could not have turned out more different. After I got married, I felt like superman! From the moment I said, 'I do,' I felt like I'd become unstoppable – as if 'S' had been planted to my chest. No goal was too big. It was totally unexplainable. As I write this, I wonder if this is something experienced by other men as I have never really broached this subject with my married male friends.

In this day and age, we are flooded with negative connotations regarding the concept of marriage. Together with an increasing number of divorces and celebrities making a total mockery of it, it is no wonder few have a respect for it. How do we maintain the most sacred of rituals? All the obvious answers come to mind - love, trust, respect... and more. For me though, there are three key aspects that are particularly important.

The first is to 'keep it fresh'. Do not stop dating because you are married. Second, do not stop evolving or challenging yourself... and each other. Finally, remember you are a team now. Every team needs balance, positive direction and definitive goals. For me these three things have been central to creating a transformational and lasting union with my wife.

Afterword

I have spoken about how I really had no intention of writing this book. However, I was driven by the fact that if I didn't do it, it would be a disservice to God. Marriage is something that I had always wanted to experience but it was only when I was in it that I realised there was so much more I could have learnt before and brought into it. It therefore made sense that at least some others felt the same, so it was important to share what I have learnt... and am still learning.

So, as with my first book, *The NAKED Truth About Having A Baby*, I have laid bare my soul, with heart on my sleeve and written about my experiences of a life event where the 'sunny picture' of the big dress and romantic ambience is similar to a photoshopped image. What we often don't speak about are the realities of what you're left to navigate in the days and years after; the joys and woes of sharing your life with someone else... forever. This is by no means meant to be a fool-proof or definitive manual for marriage. Instead, what I offer is a real, honest and personal perspective on what the components and keys to a successful marriage have been for me. In sharing them with you, I hope you can find something that will help you appreciate your union or that you can apply to make it better where it needs to be.

This book is for you, at whatever stage you are, whether man or woman, single or dating, married or divorced. There is something in here for everyone, to prepare you for, help you during, or reflect back on *The NAKED Truth About Marriage*.

[1] *Oxford Dictionary of English*, A Stevenson, Oxford University Press, 2010

[2] *The Holy Bible*, New King James Version, Ephesians 4:26

[3] *Cambridge Dictionary of English*, E Walter, Cambridge University Press, 1995

[4] *Oxford Dictionary of English*, A Stevenson, Oxford University Press, 2010

[5]https://www.visionpsychology.com/five-levels-of-intimacy/ accessed on 22 May 2020

[6] *The Holy Bible*, New King James Version, Ephesians 5:31

Author Biography

Jernine is married to Marlon Russell and together they have three children, Reiley, Rae and Roman.

For 17 years, she worked in the Criminal Justice System in varied roles within the courts, youth offending teams and prisons and probation service. Her skill set is vast and diverse having worked with young people and their families, as well as adults, in various capacities. Her focus was on providing holistic and therapeutic interventions that equip individuals with the skills to make life-affirming decisions for positive and directional changes in their lives.

One of Jernine's skills and strengths is her ability to support and empower others, and this inspired her to start She Reigns and Take the Reigns CIC, organisations that work to promote self-identity, empower, uplift and motivate women through self-development, affirmations and building self-esteem. She does this through delivering events, workshops, programmes and one-to-one work with women through coaching and mentoring. Jernine also uses her own experiences as a woman, mother and professional to inspire others.

Her first book was *The NAKED Truth About Having a Baby*.

Website   www.she-reigns.com

Email   info@she-reigns.co.uk

Instagram   @iamjerninerussell

Facebook   Jernine Russell